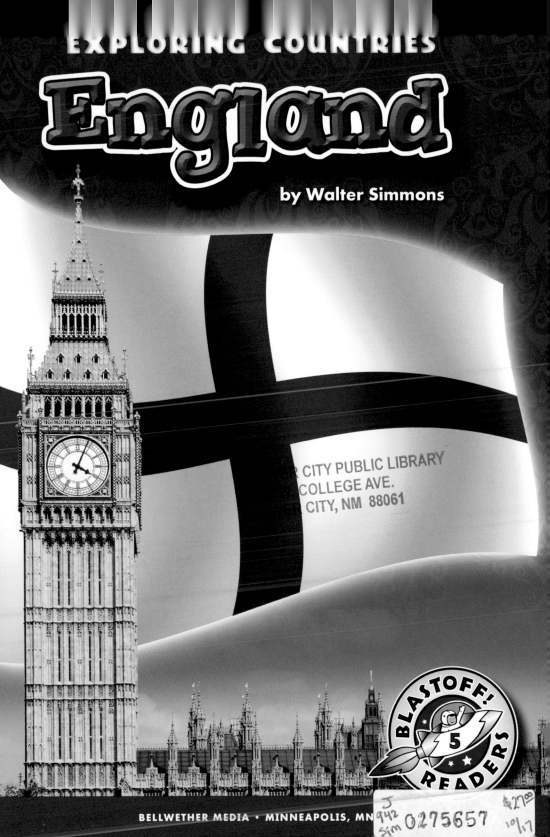

EXPLORING COUNTRIES

England

by Walter Simmons

BLASTOFF! READERS
5

BELLWETHER MEDIA · MINNEAPOLIS, MN

Note to Librarians, Teachers, and Parents:

Blastoff! Readers are carefully developed by literacy experts and combine standards-based content with developmentally appropriate text.

Level 1 provides the most support through repetition of high-frequency words, light text, predictable sentence patterns, and strong visual support.

Level 2 offers early readers a bit more challenge through varied simple sentences, increased text load, and less repetition of high-frequency words.

Level 3 advances early-fluent readers toward fluency through increased text and concept load, less reliance on visuals, longer sentences, and more literary language.

Level 4 builds reading stamina by providing more text per page, increased use of punctuation, greater variation in sentence patterns, and increasingly challenging vocabulary.

Level 5 encourages children to move from "learning to read" to "reading to learn" by providing even more text, varied writing styles, and less familiar topics.

Whichever book is right for your reader, Blastoff! Readers are the perfect books to build confidence and encourage a love of reading that will last a lifetime!

This edition first published in 2011 by Bellwether Media, Inc.

No part of this publication may be reproduced in whole or in part without written permission of the publisher. For information regarding permission, write to Bellwether Media, Inc., Attention: Permissions Department, 5357 Penn Avenue South, Minneapolis, MN 55419.

Library of Congress Cataloging-in-Publication Data

Simmons, Walter (Walter G.)
England / by Walter Simmons.
   p. cm. – (Exploring countries) (Blastoff! readers)
Includes bibliographical references and index.
Summary: "Developed by literacy experts for students in grades three through seven, this book introduces young readers to the geography and culture of England"–Provided by publisher.
ISBN 978-1-60014-479-0 (hardcover : alk. paper)
 1. England–Juvenile literature. 2. England–Social life and customs–Juvenile literature. 3. Great Britain–Juvenile literature. 4. Great Britain–Social life and customs–Juvenile literature. I. Title.
DA27.5.S55 2010
942–dc22
                                        2010011410

Printed in the United States of America, North Mankato, MN.

080110   1162

Contents

Did you know?

People can take a train between England and France. It travels through the Chunnel, which runs an average of 150 feet (46 meters) under the sea floor of the English Channel!

Atlantic Ocean

England is a country in northern Europe. It covers 50,352 square miles (130,411 square kilometers) on the southern part of the island of Great Britain. England is part of the **United Kingdom (U.K.)** and includes London, the capital city of the U.K. Northern Ireland, Scotland, and Wales are also part of the United Kingdom.

England borders Scotland to the north and Wales to the west. It also includes several small islands, such as the Isle of Wight. To the east of England is the North Sea. The **English Channel** separates England and the northern coast of France. The Irish Sea lies to the west, separating Great Britain and Ireland.

England's land is diverse and often damp from rainfall. Green river valleys, rolling hills, **wetlands**, and small mountain ranges cover the country. The Pennine Mountains and the **Lake District** are in northern England, and the Shropshire Hills and the Peak District are in the **Midlands**. The Severn River flows in a loop through the Midlands and empties into the Bristol Channel.

The English know the western reaches of their nation as the West Country. This region ends in a long **peninsula**. Waves break against the tall, rocky cliffs of Cornwall. The Fens are marshes and plains that lie in eastern England.

fun fact

Many people know the English county of Dover for its steep cliffs. The chalk in the cliffs makes them a bright white color.

fun fact

The world's first radio station operated from the Isle of Wight.

England's largest offshore island is the Isle of Wight. The Solent, a strait of the English Channel, separates the island from mainland England. The Isle of Wight has many small harbors and villages. About 130,000 people live there. In the late 19th century, England's Queen Victoria made the island famous by building her summer home there.

The Isle of Wight is also famous for its modern sporting events. Thousands of people visit the island for a motorcycle rally each year. Long-distance runners compete in the Isle of Wight Marathon. The race starts and finishes in the town of Ryde. Runners must go up and down the island's many hills.

Did you know?

The Cowes Week regatta is a sailboat race that welcomes more than 1,000 boats and their crews.

stoat

hedgehog

adder

fun fact

The adder is the only poisonous snake on the island of Great Britain.

A wide range of wildlife calls England home. Roe deer, wild goats, hedgehogs, red squirrels, and a few kinds of wildcats live in the hills and forests of northern England. The country has strict laws about hunting. This has allowed rabbits, foxes, weasels, badgers, and stoats to thrive. The stoat is a small, skinny mammal that looks like a weasel.

owl

Bird-watchers in England search the skies for owls, finches, geese, and cranes. Trout, salmon, and pike swim in England's rivers. The seas bordering England are home to dolphins, seals, and whales. On the western coasts, people sometimes spot basking sharks leaping from the sea.

Over 51 million people live in England. Many of them have **ancestors** from northern European peoples including the Celts, Saxons, Angles, Danes, and Normans.

At one time, England commanded a world empire. The nation had **colonies** in Asia, Africa, Australia, and the Americas. Many English people have roots in former colonies such as India and Jamaica.

English is the official language of England and the United Kingdom. People all over the world now speak English, which has become an international language of business and science.

Speak English Slang!

The English have some slang words that are not used in the United States. Here are some English slang words and their meanings.

English Slang	Meaning
anorak	geek
bird	woman
bloke	man
brekky	breakfast
brolly	umbrella
kip	sleep
loo	bathroom
mate	friend
quid	one pound (money)
telly	television

London Underground

fun fact

Red double-decker buses can be found on the streets of London. From the top front row, passengers get a great view of the street.

English people use buses, taxis, and trains to get from place to place. Many Londoners take the **Underground** to work. The Underground is also called the "Tube" because of the curved roofs of its train cars. Every city and small town has a **high street**. This street usually has food markets, magazine and newspaper stands, and tea shops.

Teatime is in the late afternoon. By old tradition, people stop their work and take a break. They drink a hot cup of tea with lemon or milk, and often eat a biscuit.

Where People Live in England

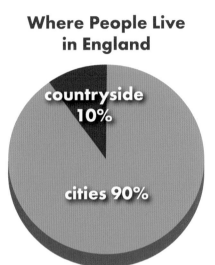

countryside 10%

cities 90%

England has thousands of **public houses**, or pubs. People visit the corner pub after dinner to talk and play games with friends and neighbors.

Going to School

All children in England must attend school from ages 5 to 16. Most children go to state schools, which are free of charge. Some parents pay for their children to attend independent schools, also called public schools.

Children go to elementary school between ages 5 and 11. They study history, geography, science, English, math, art, and music. After completing elementary school, they move on to secondary school. They have new subjects to study, including **civics**, computer technology, and foreign languages. Students who complete secondary school can apply to university. England has many universities that are hundreds of years old. Oxford University began teaching students in the late 11th century.

Did you know?

Some English children live and study at boarding schools. They return home to their families for the summer months and during breaks.

In England, city and country people have different workdays. Farmers start their day early. They work in fields of barley, oats, and wheat. Livestock farmers tend their herds of cattle or sheep. Dairy farmers work hard to make milk and cheese.

In the city, most people work in shops or offices. Many of them have **service jobs**. They work in hospitals, retail stores, restaurants, banks, and hotels. England's factories produce cars, engines, electronic equipment, and other goods.

Where People Work in England

services 80.4%

farming 1.4%

manufacturing 18.2%

Did you know?

During rush hour in England's big cities, buses, motorcycles, and cars clog the roads. Everyone drives on the left side of the road!

Did you know?

Almost 7 million English adults play a sport or exercise at least three times a week.

People in England spend their free time with friends and family, often by playing or watching sports. Soccer is the favorite sport in England. Everyone calls it football. England has some of the best football teams in the world. The English also enjoy **cricket** matches. Players pitch and hit a small ball, then sprint from one post to another to score runs. Like baseball, the game is divided into innings.

England has mountains, parks, and lakes to visit. There are many foot trails and gravel paths for hiking in the countryside. Families also enjoy taking vacations in Spain, Greece, and other countries in Europe.

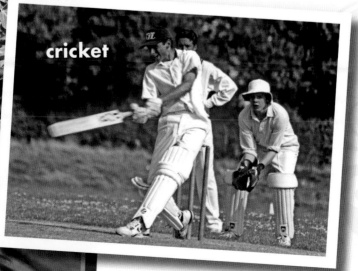

cricket

fry-up

bangers and mash

fun fact

Some English towns are world-famous for their cheese. They include Stilton and the village of Cheddar.

The English usually start the day with a hearty breakfast. The morning **fry-up** includes eggs, bacon, sausages, toast, beans, tomatoes, and mushrooms. Lunch is a time for soups, sandwiches, or warm dishes. Chipped beef is made from small pieces of dried, flavored meat covered with a sauce. Bangers and mash, or sausages and mashed potatoes, is a popular dish. English people also enjoy fish and chips, a tasty snack of fried fish and french fries.

The evening meal often features meat pie, a mix of beef or lamb and vegetables inside a piecrust. Other evening favorites are curry, rice, and pasta dishes. Roast meat and potatoes are common for the Sunday meal, called Sunday roast.

fish and chips

England has several important holidays when banks and most stores close. The English call these "bank holidays." Boxing Day is the day after Christmas. It was a tradition to give workers and servants small gifts. Today, people in England give money and food to the poor on Boxing Day.

Guy Fawkes Day takes place on November 5. In 1605, Guy Fawkes tried to blow up the Palace of Westminster with the king and **parliament** inside. Guards discovered the plot and arrested him. People celebrate the king's survival with bonfires and fireworks.

fun fact

On Guy Fawkes Day, children make Guy Fawkes dolls to burn later that night!

Did you know?

The Tower of London protects the famous crown jewels of England. They include diamonds, rubies, sapphires, pearls, and emeralds. There are 23,578 gemstones in all.

London has many landmarks that are important to English history. The Tower of London is an old fortress near the Thames River. It was built in 1078. The kings of England used it to protect themselves against riots and invasions. It also served as a prison.

Upriver from the Tower lies the Palace of Westminster, where the parliament meets. First built sometime in the 11th century, it has been restored many times. Its most famous feature is the clock tower, known as Big Ben. Today, these landmarks are symbols of national pride, reminding the English of their history and traditions.

Palace of Westminster

Stonehenge

fun fact

South of London, in the county of Wiltshire, stands a mysterious ancient monument called Stonehenge. No one knows exactly why Stonehenge was built, but many believe it was a site for sacred rituals.

Fast Facts About England

England's Flag

The flag of England shows the cross of Saint George. The cross appears in red on a white background. Saint George is the patron saint of England. English knights wore his symbol into battle in hopes that he would protect them from harm and help them defeat their enemies. The English flag makes up part of the Union flag, which stands for the entire United Kingdom.

Official Name: England

Area: 50,352 square miles (130,411 square kilometers); England is the largest country in the United Kingdom.

Capital City:	London
Important Cities:	Birmingham, Liverpool, Leeds, Manchester, Sheffield, Bristol, Leicester
Population:	51,446,000 (August 2009)
Official Language:	English
National Holiday:	Saint George's Day (April 23)
Religions:	Christian (71.6%), None or Unspecified (23.1%), Other (5.3%)
Major Industries:	farming, manufacturing, mining, services, tourism
Natural Resources:	oil, natural gas, limestone, coal, chalk, clay, farmland
Manufactured Products:	cars, food products, clothing, electronics, jet engines, steel
Farm Products:	barley, beets, oats, potatoes, wheat, sheep, cattle, cheese, milk, eggs, wool
Unit of Money:	British pound; the pound is divided into 100 pence.

Glossary

ancestors—relatives who lived long ago

civics—studies related to being a good citizen of a country or community

colonies—territories owned and settled by people from another country

cricket—a game played with a ball, bats, and low stands called wickets

English Channel—a waterway separating England and France

fry-up—a hearty, traditional English breakfast

high street—the main street of an English town or city

Lake District—a region of mountains and lakes in northern England

Midlands—a region of large cities, mines, and factories in the center of England

parliament—the group of people elected to make laws in some countries

peninsula—a section of land that extends out from a larger piece of land and is almost completely surrounded by water

public houses—neighborhood gathering places that serve food and drinks; public houses are also called pubs.

service jobs—jobs that perform tasks for people or businesses

Underground—the London subway system; Londoners often call the Underground the "Tube."

United Kingdom (U.K.)—a nation that includes England, Scotland, Wales, and Northern Ireland

wetlands—wet, spongy land; bogs, marshes, and swamps are wetlands.

To Learn More

AT THE LIBRARY
Ashman, Linda. *Come to the Castle!: A Visit to a Castle in Thirteenth-Century England*. New York, N.Y.: Roaring Brook Press, 2009.

Blashfield, Jean F. *England*. New York, N.Y.: Children's Press, 2007.

Whyte, Harlinah. *England*. New York, N.Y.: Benchmark Books, 2010.

ON THE WEB
Learning more about England is as easy as 1, 2, 3.

1. Go to www.factsurfer.com.

2. Enter "England" into the search box.

3. Click the "Surf" button and you will see a list of related Web sites.

With factsurfer.com, finding more information is just a click away.

Index

The images in this book are reproduced through the courtesy of: Juan Martinez, front cover, p. 14 (small); Maisei Raman, front cover (flag), p. 28; Jon Eppard, pp. 4-5; David Hughes, pp. 6-7; Xavier Ye, p. 6 (small); Charles Bowman/Photolibrary, p. 8; Nigel Hicks/Photolibrary, p. 9; Jill Lang, pp. 10-11; Nature Picture Library/Photolibrary, p. 10 (top); David Dohnal, p. 10 (middle); Amra Pasic, p. 10 (bottom); Pawl Libera/Photolibrary, p. 12; Martin Bond/Photolibrary, p. 14; Adam Burton/Photolibrary, p. 15; Patrick Eden/Alamy, pp. 16-17; Craig Randell/Alamy, p. 18 (left); Geanina Bechea, p. 18 (right); Tim Bewer/Photolibrary, p. 19; Daniel Bosworth/Photolibrary, pp. 20-21; Rick Strange/Alamy, p. 21 (small); Pixel Memoirs, p. 22 (top); Joe Gough, p. 22 (bottom); Peter Dazeley/Photolibrary, p. 23; Kordcom Kordcom/Photolibrary, pp. 24-25; Kenneth William Caleno, p. 24 (small); Carolyn Clarke/Alamy, p. 26; David H. Seymour, p. 27 (top); Matthew Jacques, p. 27 (bottom); imagestock, p. 29 (bill & coin).